C000102715

Don't Be a Cactus

Copyright

ISBN

Paperback: 979-8-9900379-0-8

Hardcover: 979-8-9900379-1-5

E-Book: 979-8-9900379-2-2

Publisher: Dorian S. Withrow Jr. / Withrow, LLC

List of Previous Works
Thoughts Of Creativity King 114 Realities

Thoughts Of Creativity King 114 Realities is a creative self-help book. It comprises unique free-verse poetry, illustrations, haikus, and short stories. This book aims to help people cultivate themselves and think about their existence. The goal is to inspire people to make changes within themselves and others around them. Readers contemplate forgiveness, vulnerability, social issues, and goals through free verse poetry. Illustrations bring an authentic and sincere visual aspect to the poetic work. Haikus add flavor to small implementations of imagery and meaning. The author also added short stories. These are personal stories from his life. These stories have moral and ethical lessons to help people overcome their troubles and misconceptions about life. This book took six years to produce. The work in this book comes heavily from experience. The experience comes from his own life and his perception of other people's conditions, actions, and mentalities.

Readers will learn from the author and themselves by self-examining and analyzing their reflections on their lives. This book allows people, young and old, to read something relatable. The creative components will develop the reader's cravings for more.

Wisdom 45 Advice

Wisdom 45 Advice is a book with 45 topics that touch on essential subjects such as friendship, communication, vulnerability, money, and more. The topics have an abundance of life lessons and philosophy. This book has helped people take new perspectives and steps to reach their goals. The book has illustrations and poetic elements for creative, friendly readers. Most importantly, this literature is more than just absorbing information; it is a toolbox. As readers embark on their growth journey, they will improve their ability to combat inevitable troubles like grief. You will also understand what it means to learn yourself, how to stay persistent and focused, and how to make a vision come true.

Conversations You Need

Conversations You Need is a self-help book made of dialogue and quotes. Engage in honest conversations for moral and ethical education. Learn what it is like to overcome trials and fear. What does it mean to forgive and strengthen a family? How should you approach the steps to meet your goals? How should one deal with grief or criticism? *Conversations You Need* is a fast and easy read, which is excellent for a different approach to learning. This book is perfect for anyone having a busy, sad, great, or lazy day. Anyone can pick up this book to learn and contemplate the conversations needed for self-development.

Withrow LLC

Withrow, LLC is a consulting company that helps people become authors. Its mission is to help people meet their aspirations. Participants will learn what it takes to self-publish their literature. They will gain all the necessary knowledge and resources to make their author goals come to life. Other services include speaking engagements and healing circles. Speaking engagements touch on topics of self-development, growth, and goal setting. Participants will learn what it takes to form goals, meet goals, and transform into a better self. Healing circles allow people to share a comfortable, confidential, and welcoming space for vulnerability, overcoming trauma, growth, and bonding.

"The advice is not about the other party. It is about you. We often make the mistake of thinking we are not wrong."

Mr. Dorian S. Withrow Jr.

Table Of Content

Contact

Author: Dorian S. Withrow Jr.

Social media: Instagram, Tik Tok, Twitter

- **@dswjr.18**

Website

- **www.dswjr.com**

Email

- **114realities@gmail.com**

Introduction

If you value your relationships, whether on a personal or a communal level, this book is for you. This book is a treasure trove of information you need to make the best of your connection and amend burnt bridges. I bring the knowledge I gained from my education in animal behavior ecology and conservation (ABEC) to personal growth and human relationships. From a house cat to the king of the jungle or from an ape to an elephant, there is so much ABEC can teach us on how to improve our interaction. Through reflections on my education, life lessons, and philosophy, I provide an outlook on our need to strengthen our relationships. There are a variety of topics that apply and supplement our relationships. These topics also apply to general interactions with everyday people. The literature will engage in subjects such as play, communication, relationship rules, altruism, learning yourself, etc. As you read, internalize the lessons to determine how it applies to your life and the lives of others around you. Every reader can gain perspective by utilizing tools that assist them in improving the quality of their interactions. Don't go just yet, one last thing! I want us to work together. Learning is a cooperative act. Talk to me. I placed pages for you to put your thoughts on. Give your responses to me, critique me, and tell me whether you agree. I want to know what you like and do not like. Let us have a conversation.

Personal Message

We all have problems in our relationships. These relationships can be incredible teachers for self-development. My problem was bringing some of the old negative experiences to the present. The concept of control was something I needed help with. I also needed help with maintaining trust. These issues were not extreme or causing harm, but they were blocking my connection. The connection block reduced the longevity of the relationships. They were good and meaningful relationships, but to take it a step further, something was missing. Initially, when I acknowledged my issues, I chose to outlearn my problem. I read and watched anything I could to reach the perfect balance to let connection happen.

Learning took me, but so far. It helped, but I needed something more. Eventually, I went to counseling. As I am typing this out, I am on my fourth session. I needed to acknowledge that I was having difficulty reaching connection on my end. I then sought to make an effort to change. The change

was for someone other than my partner, family, or
friends. The change was only for one person: the
person that mattered most, me. I called the
counseling office at my school and asked to speak
to a counselor. I was surprised to find out how this
process would go. We will refer to the individual
who answered the call as an office person. They
asked a variety of questions about my background
and experiences. I was comfortable answering them.
The questions were necessary to gauge my needs.
We reviewed a lot of information regarding why I
wanted counseling, such as location, scheduling,
laws, and more. Eventually, the call was over. After
some time, I received an email from my counselor.
The email had an intake form to assess anything
else important. This form is required for the
counseling appointment. It helps the counselor
better understand who they are working with. After
completing the form, I received more information
about the meeting time, location, and place. We
agreed upon a time to meet on campus. My first
appointment was set.

I needed the bravery to head out and step into the office on the appointment day. I needed the courage to express my problems and needs to a stranger. I accomplished that with ease. It would be best if you were vulnerable to get the most out of getting help and improving your life. You need to lack the fear of speaking frankly, unfiltered speech, and to talk clearly. I talked with the counselor about my trust problem and need for control. I also mentioned my concerns about developing a better relationship with my father. So far, I have shifted my perspective regarding what I can control to improve my trust. I am a person who is strong-willed and attempting to become the best I can be. I applied what I learned in the therapy sessions to my interactions with my partner. Over the past month, I have made improvements in building my trust and changing my concept of what I find acceptable. My current objective is to create a better bond with my father.

I encourage others to do the same. What bothers you? What troubles you every day? What

thoughts cause you pain? These are the very
questions I asked myself. These questions helped
me shift my mind on getting help. How long do you
want to live with this? Do not purposely prevent
yourself from reaching happiness. The quality of
your days is paramount. This advice is not only
about you but the people you interact with. You
influence your environment. You have an impact on
people. Make changes and watch your inner work
emit transformation you hadn't conceived. This
book is a stepping stone to reach your goal.

Do you have a personal message?

Inferences & Observation

One major yet small fundamental lesson I
learned in the ABEC program was observation and
inference. We need to know the difference between
the two. Observation is an act of visually analyzing
whatever objective you set to study. An inference is
making a proposition or judgment about an
observation with bias. I pose a hypothetical example
of an observation I made for bird watching. When
watching a bird, I noted that it raised its head three
times and lowered it three times. I saw it move its
wings vertically up and down in sequence three
times. The bird lifted its left leg twice every four
consecutive steps. The bird then chirped and sang. I
only described what I saw without the addition of
my opinion. Through observation, someone may
make the inference that the bird is injured. They
could say the bird is attempting to take flight,
although it can not because of an injured leg. This is
an inappropriate judgment. The bird could be
performing anything, such as a mating display. We
can not ask the bird what it is doing or the meaning

of its actions. We analyze its actions and try to find some logical explanation for the behavior through context, associations, and research. We can go down the wrong path when we make inferences in a conservation or ecological context. People may prescribe inappropriate treatment for animals or the environment due to misinformation. When it comes to our relationships or everyday people, we must observe our partners. We have to watch our partners with an objective lens. We need to do so without inferences because we can be very wrong. For example, when a wife is observed talking less, the husband may infer that his wife lacks interest in their relationship. Although it could be possible, it is not confirmed to be true. Previous experience could be the cause of his inference. The inference may be assumed because the wife has done something like this to her friend. This inference also holds bias, and it is under false judgment. Her reason for the behavior is currently unknown. We can not keep the assumption that there is a relationship issue due to previous experience.

Through an account of external factors, we may discover that the partner lost their job, argued with a family member, or was dealing with illness. We come closer to understanding that the relationship has no friction.

Lastly, there is a concept called anthropomorphism, which is a big no-no in animal behavior. Anthropomorphism applies human-like characteristics to non-human creatures. Here, I provide an example of a bad chimpanzee experience and its connection to anthropomorphism. Visitors view a chimpanzee "smiling and happy" to see a child banging on the enclosure glass at the zoo (very bad). Before this, the chimpanzee had been harassed and physically harmed by other chimpanzees within a zoo enclosure. For those of us who are unaware of what the "smile" is, the chimpanzee is not smiling. The chimp is expressing what is called a fear grimace. It is an outward physical display of discomfort and aggression.

In this way, imposing our characteristics or attributes can be problematic for other species and ourselves. If we misinterpret behavior and signs, we may provide improper measures to improve their well-being. Those with exotic animals like small primates often misinterpret facial expressions, bringing many fatal consequences. A small primate's "smile" has led to many bad smiles. We can not "anthropomorphize" our fellow humans, but we can project ourselves upon others. That means we attribute our emotions, thoughts, and capabilities to others. When we do this to others, it can be detrimental to the relationship. We all have different experiences, ideas, emotional control, and capabilities. Therefore, we may set too high or too low expectations when we project. We may apply too much pressure on others. There can be a lack of consideration for others' emotional state and way of thinking. Projection bleeds into another's goals, self-esteem, approaches to life, boundaries, communication, and so on. Do your best to avoid projection towards your partner. You can be in the wrong and move away from the path of a proper solution.

What are your thoughts?

Ethograms

Ethograms are an essential tool for studying an animal's frequency of behavior. We use ethograms to track various activities: behavior in play, feeding, socialization, and mating. Ethograms help monitor specific behavior of animals to distinguish changes like abnormalities and to determine what is influencing them. The behaviors are defined from the start, tallied, and timed. As we strive to become the best we can be, I think creating something like an ethogram for ourselves is beneficial. You can make your personal development tracker. We all have habits, ways of thinking, and responses to our environment. Track yourself through a chart every day. If you have a terrible habit or detrimental thoughts, try to track that.

How many times have you had negative thoughts? How many times have you bit your fingernails? When you perform such behavior or think of specific ideas, knowing what triggers it and the circumstances around it is relevant. An argument can lead to behavior such as nail biting because it creates stress. You may have wrong thoughts when doing math homework because of the intense pressure your parents put on you to improve. When a behavior is performed enough times, it becomes habitual or a way of being. Many say, "This is just how I am and what I do." We can run the risk of going down the poor path of complacency and acceptance. It is significant to become very self-aware of what we are doing. Monitor yourself through your body and thoughts. The good thing about the personal development tracker is that it allows us to see progress or not. If the last time you bit your nails was over three days ago instead of every day, then we are getting somewhere. The same applies to poor thoughts and emotions. I track my emotions throughout the day. I write about why I was happy, sad, angry, and so on. The most relevant component of this personal development chart is my response to emotion and circumstance. When I write my response to the situation, I can then see if I am responding better to

negative emotions, reducing destructive behaviors
and thinking negative thoughts. I am on my way to
a better me. Ethograms helped me. I became more
self-aware of how unaware of my emotions I am.
I'd say that when it comes down to dealing with
problems in my life, the only things that come to
my mind are solutions. I did not measure my
internal state. It is like walking in the cold for a long
time. You feel it and maybe conscious that you are
experiencing it in the back of your mind, but after
some time during the walk, you do not consciously
acknowledge the cold feeling on your face or legs. I
used to track my emotions through the day
according to what happened and how I responded.
The hardest part about that process sometimes was
acknowledging the feelings and the circumstances
at times as well. Even worse, how I handled
something that threw me into turmoil. It brought me
great self-awareness. We like to think we are better
than we actually are.

    Along with self-awareness, I followed
continuous action to change responses and

emotions. (On a bit of a stoic journey.) My biggest lesson is accepting who I am instead of running from it and remaining stagnant. I have done a lot of interviews, and being reasonably vulnerable is easy for me. It helps a lot with dealing with challenging situations and circumstances. It allowed me to recall the most difficult times and maintain an excellent internal state. I became much more resilient because of it. My only critique of myself would be finding someone instead of a piece of paper at times. It could have changed something.

What would you track?

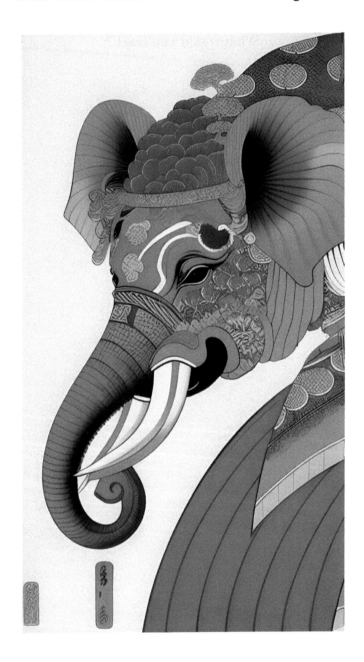

Adaptation

An adaptation in the animal behavior world
is a heritable trait shaped by natural selection,
which enhances the ability to survive and
reproduce. Animals gain mechanisms to improve
their survival through danger, death, reproduction,
and learning. Humans aren't different from our
animal friends in many ways. As humans, we also
deal with death, reproduction, danger, and constant
learning. Thinking of all this can be daunting yet it
is what transforms us. However, humans do differ in
one significant way. Our capability to obtain
information and use it is unique. Knowledge is vital
to our success. When learning is internalized,
intentionally applied, and brought out through
behavior, it allows manifestation. If you repeat the
behavior enough, it will become ingrained into your
thinking and body. In essence, we can change when
we know better and do better. Always strive to
learn, but learn what is effective and positive. I
emphasize that you learn from someone
knowledgeable about your goals. Go to people that

have done it or are doing it. When we make
changes, we are better for society, our group, and
our relationships. We benefit our families, friends,
and even the strangers we may see only once. Let
now be the time if you need a kick in the behind to
make some changes. The certainty of manifesting
one's goals through thought alone is very slim. Your
goal could be anything, such as working on anger,
self-esteem, business, or academics; it is simply
about taking action. Start at any point; make sure to
start. We often know that something within us needs
to change, but lack the willpower to start. Find that
source or reason to become better. When we begin,
we have to be consistent. Unfortunately, what is
good or better for our well-being is often
overshadowed by what we favor more intensely. We
need to train ourselves by constantly behaving and
thinking of priority first. If you need to eat better,
continuously, but slowly build up your endurance to
consume healthier options. Add more of what is
necessary to your plate gradually. Sometimes we
need to just leap in head first. The first jump is

always the bravest milestone if you're considering things that will help you advance. Condition your mind by reminding yourself of how necessary your self-improvement is. Also, acknowledge that you are making progress.

Furthermore, there are billions of people on earth. Someone fits your shoes very well. Find people who have struggled and overcome things you are attempting to triumph over. Seek them out and ask many questions. The most important thing to do is act. Do what you can to improve yourself for your community, family, and partner.

How will you adapt?

Media & Perception

In my animal behavior class, we discussed nature versus nurture in the context of dog breeds. This distinction is essential for the legislation on specific dog breeds. There is a debate about the variety of restrictions placed against certain breeds and not against others. Some politicians and communities believe that particular characteristics and behaviors threatening the public are part of certain breeds' nature. Some factors influence this public perception. Through newspapers, radio, and television, the media portrays certain breeds as dangerous and unruly. There are ethical issues associated with this. The breeds are restricted through bias in housing, locations, etc. Breeds distinguished as aggressive have been discriminately documented for inflicting property damage and prone to violence against people (and other animals). Some people believe it is in their "nature" to be savage and bring harm. Some people think dogs have an intrinsic attribute of violence.

Some people who opposed the restrictions said that dogs are nurtured into violence and disobedience. The dogs are trained, isolated from human contact, and bred to guard, protect, and fight. These people believe that some breeds have environmental factors that promote violence. Ultimately, when the conversation about nature vs nurture comes up, it is a combination of both. The media needs to help produce a good image. Certain breeds are portrayed in the media with negative connotations and denunciations. Media is a powerful tool for providing a message and influencing the public's perception. The stereotypes about some dog breeds can relate to groups of people in some ways. I believe that human behavior is nurtured or learned. Our environment assists in directing our way of thinking and behavior. There are often laws and restrictions that target people, often minorities. Some people are said to be more likely to engage in harmful conduct or crime due to their environmental risk factors. Groups of people are portrayed in the media to suit a terrible narrative.

The narrative trickles down and aids the
reinforcement of negative ideas or generalizations.
Lamentably, the narrative infiltrates and manifests
stronger within the targeted group. Those same
groups, within their circles, impose self-destructing
narratives upon each other. Internalizing the
narratives allows evil thoughts to pollute someone's
thinking about others like them and themselves.
There are well-designed restrictions on some groups
of people. There are restrictions on housing,
demographic locations, work opportunities, job
placement, and so much more. To improve, we must
change how we nurture, shifting the poor narrative
imposed on people and the ideology spread amongst
themselves. As a society, we often take information
at face value without a deeper dive. We have to
combat the narrative by making our own through
positive relationships. We can change the
environment around us by maintaining good
connections. Follow a mentor or philosophical or
religious guidelines to help you approach a better
way of appreciating or loving. Relationships are the

foundation of the community and its strength. They provide opportunity and progress by unifying resources for better living conditions. Most significantly, in this regard, we need to take hold of positive media that portrays the progressive, stellar aspects of love in our communities. The media is always more effective when it is close to home. Whether the small or grand scale of work, it is all-important.

What are ways we can change media?

Habituation

Habituation is an excellent concept to keep in mind. To be habituated means a lack of response to a stimulus. A stimulus causes a reaction within us, like a static shock or startling buzzer. If you live near a firehouse where trucks are continuously moving and setting off sirens, you'll hear them initially, but at some point, you will no longer notice the siren. When you find that someone put a lot of cologne or perfume on for a special occasion, it first smells strong, but after a while, the smell fades. Your brain takes in so much information that it must discern what is more important at any given time. Attention is away from something causing stimulation (a strong smell) for an extended period. Habituation varies from person to person. Some things take more getting used to than others. You can become habituated to video games, smells, enticing visuals, and touch. When it comes to the troubles of the world and concerns in our personal lives, we can also become habituated or tolerant. When a risk factor (like gun violence, drugs, domestic abuse) is in our presence long enough, some of us accept it or ignore it. In this sense, habituation is detrimental to building one's self and taking steps in the right direction to resolve problems that don't have to exist. Being numb to troubles applies to relationships, education, hospitals, finances, and more. We avoid habituation by discipline and maintaining a sense of duty. More importantly, do this for yourself. Do not ignore the issues as we feel, hear, see, and think of the changes happening. Do not allow it to become acceptable. Do not become tolerant of it. To do this, one must reduce the fear of consequences. One has to stand one's ground to improve what one touches.

Should we become numb to problems?

Altruism

Altruism is a behavior that benefits the receiver while bringing no benefit to the provider. I can't entirely agree with this definition, but we will see the disagreement later. Here is an example of altruism. Prairie dogs will shout alarm calls to their fellows in their vicinity. The alarm call alerts other prairie dogs to get away. The calls match the predator type (bird, dog, or snake). The other prairie dogs will go into the appropriate hiding spaces. The heroic risk taker making the call has increased its risk of predation. The other prairie dogs will have a better chance of survival. Another case of altruism involves chimpanzees. The provider will groom the receiver's skin. Grooming provides the receiver comfort by ridding themselves of bugs, mites, and dirt.

The acts of the provider may seem to be at their deficit. What do they get? The alarm caller is at greater risk of being in harm's way. The chimpanzee grooming the other does not receive any reciprocity. I believe this to be untrue. The prairie dog performing the alarm call educates others to serve the same behavior when necessary. The others will achieve the behavior that could benefit the caller later. When the prairie dog alerts relatives to go into hiding, he attempts to preserve his gene pool.

Furthermore, the chimpanzee that grooms is lining itself up to receive some help later on. At times, the service is not reciprocated, so they may not engage in altruism between the two individuals. That is ok! The chimpanzee gets some practice. There is a social learning component as well. Other members of the group might have noticed and followed suit. The chimpanzee increases its chance of getting groomed by performing in front of others. The members may provide this "grooming" in exchange for food, care, protection, and grooming. As people, we are not much different. In the context of altruism, people's behavior will have some cost. The cost can come in time, money, emotion, energy, and physicality. We sometimes engage in altruistic behavior for the benefit of our kin and friends with no expectations. Occasionally, we do this because of the relatability and intensity of the connection. Some people do not seek to benefit anyone. Strangers often get the short stick because of our viewpoint of people outside our circles. This kind of perspective can limit our generosity, potential connection, and service to the community.

I want to help us battle our individuality. A collectivist mind is crucial because it means cooperation. Having a collectivist mind means valuing the group over self or individual needs. To incorporate a collectivistic mindset, we must avoid seeking benefits when providing for someone else. Let your generosity be from the purity of your compassion and kindness. People only sometimes deliver on their end. If there is an unexpected expectation for the receiver, then it is immoral of us to dictate when we want to receive back. We can not pressure people in that way because it causes tension in the relationship and it molds your interactions in the future. If you absolutely must receive benefits, change how you think about it.

You may have increased your generosity. You improve someone's outlook on certain people or strangers in general. You could have indirectly stopped them from self-harming or harming others. You kept someone from starving. You shifted someone's narrative on life. You helped someone overcome injustice. You influenced their day, even momentarily, and made it delightful. There will be a significant change in your character for the better when you benefit others, gradually. There may also be concern over the weight of both giving and receiving. I respond that what you grow into is more remarkable than giving and receiving. It is better to stay on the positive side of reciprocity. You can put more wisdom into your thoughts according to any situation that will help you gain. No matter what you do for someone, you will also benefit. Prosocial behavior, to help someone else regardless of what happens to yourself, allows your relationships, reputation, and community to thrive. This is about you becoming something great, yet not to your detriment. Being prosocial does not mean emptying yourself until you have nothing. Find your balance. Seeing this way is about limiting the view of someone else as a transaction and individualistic path of thinking.

Can you do for others without receiving anything back?

Conflict Resolution

No matter the position, age, or status of people, the relationship will have some conflict at some point. When there is conflict, we must suppress negative qualities. Spite and selfishness are very harmful to forging and maintaining relationships. When we are spiteful, we do things detrimental to both parties. It is one thing to bring someone else misfortune, but it will worsen your character. Selfishness is a double-edged sword. To be selfish is only to consider oneself regarding consequences. Our relationships fall apart when we hold these two negative qualities in our approach to desired outcomes. Without conflict resolution, we reduce the quality and quantity of our relationships. Alternatively, people should develop short-term and long-term goals to find the motivation to cooperate. Cooperation may mean reducing one's pride and ego for agreeableness. Pride and ego can prevent us from seeing the light at the end of the tunnel. They limit our ability to connect in a meaningful way. It can prevent us from learning and being compassionate. Suppressing our negative qualities entails self-examination, understanding, and compromising for the greater good. An essential way of guiding conflict resolution is the equity approach. Everyone gets what they need. We all know everything will be complex. This method does not necessarily mean "giving" but seeking mutual respect, compliance, and understanding. It means you emit the better qualities you have. It is not to say become a doormat or pushover. It is favorable to seek such equitability in an outcome. The best resolutions come when both parties are satisfied.

When equity is lacking, we must employ a cooperative mind that helps us overcome such a hurdle. Again, cooperate on both sides so that eventually there is no "side." People can have opposing viewpoints, all while maintaining cooperation. Avoid loud, turbulent shouting matches. Do not seek to "one up," outsmart, or be boastful because it brings about escalation and unnecessary tension. Also, attempt to be conscious of gestures and physical appearance in an altercation. Ask yourself, do I appear as a threat? Is what I'm doing working for the betterment of us? These conflict resolution tools are not to be used for selfishness or gaining an advantage but for amending relationships and improving bonds. Conflict resolution is important because it concerns you and what you can become when everything is said and done. I am on the journey of having as few regrets as possible. I remember conflicts I could have handled differently. I understand my negative qualities, the stuff that blocks unification. There are bridges I wish to cross again. People are much more valuable than our temperament. Considering others and seeking a win for everyone is not always easy, but it is worthwhile. One of my biggest regrets is becoming or doing what I did not like in other people. You lose a piece of yourself that you might spend a lifetime trying to regain. That is why it is best to resolve conflicts. Avoid burning bridges. Stop dwelling on what will taint your character.

What negative qualities can you change?

Coevolution

When we think of evolution, we think of change. Evolution, in the biological context, means descent with modification. Descent with modification means animals gain different traits over generations. Some of us may think of it as something that just happens. Although it doesn't just "happen." Various influences, such as natural selection, selective mating, and other ecological factors, promote such evolution. We need to "evolve" when we are involved in human relationships. I want to think of our evolution differently. Let us look at evolution as "change" for us. Like a butterfly, we go through metamorphosis. Or we make changes when we metaphorically die and become reborn. When reborn, we lose an old way of thinking, behavior, or habit. By taking on something new, we make a change. We shed our old skin and display new skin. What causes change within someone is information internalized and acted upon. All the information from our environment is not far away, but it is up to us to shape, keep, and use it effectively.

Within our relationships, be that person to help people evolve. Another type of evolutionary concept is mutualistic coevolution. Mutualistic coevolution is when two species have processes that benefit each other. We can take the example of bees and flowers. The flowers provide nectar for the bees. Bees spread pollen, allowing more flowers to grow. Evolution in our relationships happens when we are mutualistic—being mutualistic means receiving benefits from both parties. How can we grow without challenging each other? We ought to sharpen each other. We can help mold each other into becoming a better person. We have to hold each other accountable. We must confront each other's morals and values to determine what is in the best interest of ourselves and all parties. To help someone else improve, we have to be devoid of selfishness; we have to give information or resources for the betterment of someone else. We need to educate each other instead of battling and finding fault. In reshaping yourself or another person, sometimes we have to be antagonistic, too. Sometimes, to help someone, we must be seemingly non-beneficial to them for them to benefit. We may need to question a detrimental way of thinking and living. We have to prevent them from acting out destructive behaviors and guide them into something more healthy. We may have to withhold certain information or resources. Attempting this brings positivity in many ways for both sides. Even if the road is long and hard to help another person, you train yourself to look within your actions, learn new things, and help yourself. Change will invade other areas of life. Amongst difficulties, within the process, seek a win for both sides.

How can you help someone help themselves?

Play

Within animal behavior, play is an integral part of development. The play improves survival by practicing hunting, learning social signals, and the group's rules. Some animals engage in social play. When young, lions display hunting behaviors with littermates as they play. The cubs reenact hunting behaviors like lunging and biting towards the neck. The play prepares them for what will sustain them later on. Some animals play by themselves. Macaques are fond of tombstoning; they leap from high places into small bodies of water. Ravens will rotate and roll in the snow. Other animals play with objects. The Japanese macaques make and hold snowballs, and baboons play with stones. The play has its downside because the animals can injure themselves or each other. It takes away from what is important to them, such as hunting and foraging. There is also a lack of vigilance for predators when they play. Aspects of non-human animal play can relate to humans in many ways. For our human relationships, social play is relevant for learning from each other at any age. We develop a sense of social signals for appropriate interactions in our relationships. We learn the limitations of each other's temperament, joy, pain, arousal, and sensitivity. We get to observe unordinary aspects of each other. Our vigilance, like animals, is also reduced. Our surroundings disappear, and we are engaged in our activities. We become focused on each other. There is much more to discover about ourselves and the people around us. Depending on the play activity, we improve our health, social capital, and many more subtle benefits. We play when we engage in sports, card games, martial arts, video games, and more. But beware, too much play can take away from the crucial things (personal growth, social issues...). Lastly, play provides a space to show good character. People can see our best and worst qualities. We can show people what bad behavior looks like or teach others good conduct or sportsmanship in any activity.

In what ways can you use play to build better relationships?

List of Five

In the animal welfare space, there are five freedoms. The freedoms allow animals to receive humane treatment under human care. In animal welfare, we want animals to have safe and nourishing lives. We should all seek the welfare of the creatures we share this planet with. We can set a similar list of five freedoms for our relationships. When we apply the five freedoms, we want freedom from whatever particular harm there could be. The five freedoms in the human context aim to set parameters around improving our treatment of each other. What are the five freedoms you desire for your interactions with others? We apply freedoms to what we value: Freedom from dishonesty, inauthenticity, violence, dishonor, and unacceptance. What does all that mean? Freedom to be truthful and without deceit. Freedom to have authentic expression. That is to be yourself unfiltered or untainted by society's standards. Freedom to experience nonmaleficence, to experience no mental or physical harm. Freedom from dishonor, having a good reputation for yourself, respecting one another, and letting your relationship be a privilege. Freedom of acceptance is an open-ended concept for me in the context of relationships. Accept your partner for who they are, but accept change as well. Accept the challenges that come and the differences you have that can also change. Develop your list of five freedoms that will enhance your interactions with others and everyone's well-being.

Relationships: What are your five freedoms?

Communication

Animals have many communication signals that inform others in their population and about food sources. Bioluminescent bacteria communicate through chemicals that allow them to glow. The light attracts fish, and the bacteria will reside inside and consume it. The black drum fish uses a loud sound to attract female counterparts. Whales use low-frequency calls to communicate. Bats use echolocation to detect their environment and potential prey. Wolves and bears have a fantastic sense of smell they use to find resources and others of their species many miles away. Skates use active electroreception. Electroreception is simply using an electrical output to stun prey to make hunting easier. These methods of communication allow information to be transferred from one to another.

As humans, we are not too different. We use sight, smell, sound, and touch to evaluate others. To succeed in life and gain the best interaction, we must use all those senses and others not mentioned. The information we receive from our senses can help us engage others most effectively for everyone's benefit. When we see someone else, we can judge their state of being. The clothes they wear may have an expression of some sort, whether it be of their emotional state, ideology, etc. We can see that life may be treating them well or harshly. We can see their way of thinking. We can observe bags under someone's eyes to tell they have not slept well. We can hear the tone of their voice and word choice. Through sound, we can gauge someone's thought processes and well-being. What does someone smell like? Smells can tell us about a person. The smell could be a conversation starter for what kind of food they like. Scents can trigger memories, good or bad. We learn more about the individual and people as we take in this information.

Using our senses can help us develop a big picture. We have to pay attention to what signals people are giving off. There is a problem with the big picture. When looking at the big picture, we can miss the fine points, which are the things that make up a person's inner qualities, the stuff we can't see—the more important parts of us as individuals. Therefore, we have to zoom in. We will not always be correct as humans are varying, complex creatures. We will often judge incorrectly. We must be able to locate critical components of someone to make the most of our interactions. Finding the small details can resolve conflict and tension, improve persuasion, enlighten, and more.

We can employ the cocktail party effect. The concept of the cocktail party effect is merely picking out something distinguishable from distractions. For example, in a mall, a mother can pick out her child's voice even around an enormous crowd. The mother can detect her child's voice over all other sounds. We must pick out the distinguished sign(s) from another person. Signals might mean the intention behind their words, the position of their hands, the movement of their feet, tone of voice, word choice, and so on. We can tap into the world of another person. We can build closer, stronger bonds. We can invoke better communication by

developing an understanding of people through our
senses and applying the cocktail party concept.

How have you used your sense to learn about someone?

Managing Environment

I had a zoo animal management class, and it was a great experience. That class was my first group-based class. We were assigned a task to develop a theoretical zoo. We needed to search for the animals, their habitats, diet, enrichment, and more. We needed to use that research to create an artificial habitat. There were many lessons I learned during this time. Teamwork was the biggest lesson. We applied effective communication to meet the standards and expectations. We each had parts we needed to fulfill and decided to take on. Maintaining our duty is essential because if someone takes on more work than another, there is usually conflict. Fairness is understood; people have an even share of work and stick to it. Fairness is only sometimes the case. At times, some individuals took on extra work to maintain effectiveness. If a person became sick, was dealing with grief, or had a setback, we had to pick up each other's work to complete the project. Work is not always even. The concept of equitability is much more realistic and ideal. In this case, to be equitable means everyone taking on different quantities of work to benefit everyone. It is better to have an equitable distribution of work. As for disagreements and mistakes, the group was good at addressing the issues. Conflict can lead to the breakdown of the groups and the quality of work.

Our group reflected good conflict resolution. We were equitable in completing tasks. We sought understanding from each other and even gave reassurance for setbacks. The group members were agreeable and easy to work with so we did not have difficulty meeting our requirements. Moreover, while working on the project, we needed to understand the animals we were making an enclosure for; we needed knowledge of animal behavior to know what is ideal for their needs. These experiences can be applied to relationships. We need to understand each other to create the best environment for our relationships to flourish. We can only take steps to relieve issues and prevent problems through understanding each other. Also, within our relationships, we have to focus on our designated assignments. The parts (individual) must fulfill their purpose to complete the whole (relationships). We depend upon each other, so picking up some of someone else's load is necessary for the connections to function well. Be strong where they are weak and allow other's strengths to aid where you are lacking. Groups that do poorly on assignments lack communication, competence, persistence, and, maybe most importantly, the amount of necessary care. Another significant part of group-based classes is that sometimes, the grade is collective. Everyone's grades are bound and affected by each other. One's actions bleed into everyone else. Their performance impacts their grade point average (GPA), analogous to life's overall success. We all matter to each other. When we act in our relationships and interactions, it is not only about yourself but everyone involved, even the people you do not think of.

**Have you compensated for someone's
shortcomings?**

S.A. & C / I & I

Actions have consequences. Obvious right? We learn about this at home from a very early age. I learned about causality in my animal cognition class. I learned about different species' ability to determine if they knew their actions led to some consequence. Causality is simply understanding a relationship between an aspect of an event and its outcomes. For humans, self-awareness is vital to maintaining a personal connection and understanding of causality. Your actions or words affect not only others, but you, too. Whether your actions or words are good or bad, there will be change. You change the way you view an approach to life. You manipulate the way you interact with others in the future. You change the way you think, what you feel, and how you behave. Whether the change is good or not is another concern. To be self-aware, we must self-examine. Self-examination encompasses monitoring your thoughts, emotions, and behavior. It is self-questioning and authentically emptying yourself to observe the truth without a filter. Another way of understanding causality is by engaging other people's perceptions.

Sometimes, we should understand the other person's interpretation of our actions and words. We often put little thought into this. Understanding ourselves and others will solve a lot of issues. First, you should ask. Not everyone is very outspoken, nor will people always display behaviors that indicate their thoughts and emotions. When applying the concept of observation and using appropriate interpretations, you can get closer to understanding how and why someone may have reacted to your actions or words. Next, we can use both imitation and insight when confrontation comes. When someone offends, people tend to want others or the offender to feel like they did. Essentially, the person performs imitation. The person uses imitation to retaliate by reproducing the words or actions the offended used to cause harm. People sometimes do this to stop any behavior from happening again or get vengeance. It is a way to redeem honor and bring back emotional stability. There is a desire to make the offender understand the causality of their action and self-awareness. Imitation brings a mirror to the offender or a reflection of the victim. We can use imitation to our advantage. Why not imitate the stunning example of someone who strives to seek peace?

Be a model for others to battle slander, yelling, gestures, and potential threats. It takes trial and error. When we fall short, we should get back up and try our best to stay on track. We need to have insight to gain more success than error. Insight is another way we can reduce errors when a trial arises. Insight is having the ability to see what might happen with likelihood intuitively. If you can foresee something going wrong when you behave or communicate, you have a chance to prevent more significant problems. Insight improves self-awareness, although self-awareness is a long grueling process. It is challenging to be conscious of everything we do and examine how it will affect others. We must do our best to improve for our own sake, and a higher quality of relationships will follow. The progression for better relationships involves both parties. No matter how great you build your ship to stay afloat, the ship won't move far with an lowered anchor.

What are ways you build your self awareness?

Control

There were many impactful conversations in my animal ethics and zoo animal management classes. One debate in both classes is about whether animals should be in zoos and sanctuaries. Ultimately, based on what we know, we wanted to determine if animals should be in them. Whether an advocate of zoos and sanctuaries or opposed to it, there are good points for either side. People who argue against zoos and sanctuaries say animals can not express their natural behaviors. The spaces the animals occupy lack authenticity compared to their natural habitat. Also, these animals are involuntarily on display for people, people kind or unkind. Some animals suffer being in zoos and sanctuaries. Initially, zoos were primarily for entertainment. Moreover, people who advocate for zoos and sanctuaries tend to bring up aspects of animal healing, animal safety, public education, and animal rehabilitation. The zoos and sanctuaries allow animals to thrive where, in the wild, they would have difficulty. Now, there are zoos, sanctuaries for injured and endangered animals, and entertainment.

There is a good amount of complexity in these arguments. Neither is inherently wrong. Both sides have understandable points. These two different outlooks on freedom or control apply to our human relationships. Our relationships are comparable to the pro-zoo/sanctuaries and anti-zoo/sanctuaries argument. We can make the zoo walls analogous to rules for us humans. We all have rules for our relationships, whether spoken, unspoken, or written. In our relationships, we seek our benefit, but when there are rules, we must compromise. We may hate regulations because they can smother us, restrict us, and prevent us from doing what we want to do. It limits our freedom and expression to others or the world. With rules, our authenticity is molded into something disingenuous. Without constraints, we fall to hurting each other. We have no guidelines to maintain and build relationships. There is an increased chance of surprise harm and miscommunication. Rules can raise the quality of connections. Rules ensure both parties benefit. The rules are (should be) meant to prevent damage, but they are only sometimes viewed that way. Whether rule or no rule, neither is inherently flawed. We ought to understand ourselves, our partners, and our community. Through experience and agreement, we can guide ourselves to developing great relationships. Honest and transparent communication is essential for any human connection to thrive.

Is there a need for rules or no need for rules?

Isolation

There are so many solitary animals. The wolverine, sunfish, axolotl, moose, tarantula, and skunk are all solitary predators. Fortunately, they are structured to be this way. They are suited for such a life. As isolated as they are, they still need others to assist them with parenting, survival, and food. We may think we are solitary like these animals listed. Is it ideal? We can believe that we are better off without others. We may think we have no one to count on. We may maintain the idea that no one is in our corner. That is very untrue! When we think deeply about ourselves and our condition, we find that it is us. You think you have no one because you manufactured it that way, intentionally or unintentionally. We all have choices, and many people are around to help, from organizations to support groups, places of worship, non-profit facilities, companies, government resources, etc. We may have friends and family we often refuse to ask for help or ignore. There are a ton of reasons someone may refuse to ask. Regardless, it is easier to move something big with two hands. It is easier to grab something with all five fingers. It is easier to run with two legs. We have the best balance when we have all ten toes. For us to function at our maximum potential, nothing can stand alone. Why is anything different with life challenges and difficult circumstances? We can overcome challenges alone, but it does not have to be that way. With the help of another person, anyone can get things done in less time. The weight of a burden will become lighter. No one is perfect when it comes to seeking help. I failed a class because I didn't want tutoring. I had my clothes soaked in the rain, starved when I could have eaten. I stumbled and fell on my head. There are a few concepts to help us adjust that will make receiving help much more effortless.

Pride, at times, is a terrible thing. Pride makes us want to appear better than we are. Pride leads us to avoid seeking help. Pride will set fire to our bridges (relationships/connections). We have to humble ourselves to get to where we need to be. A lot of things regarding our capabilities are out of reach. Another important concept that can hold us back is strength. Most people want to be strong, not in muscle, but in terms of endurance, resilience or tolerance. How much can you take? How much can you handle? An inadequate conception of strength will tell you, "I do not need help. I can do it on my own." You will go through many more unnecessary self-imposed troubles and misfortune. What should we think? Be humble and reconsider the concept of strength.

Acknowledge and accept not all things have to be done the hard way. There is an easier route we often miss. Strength is thinking more creatively. Why do we stick to two options as problems arise when so many solutions exist? Strength is going beyond dichotomy. We have to think of strength as the ability to be vulnerable and humble. We need the courage to ask and the bravery to receive. Strength is having the guts to fight our self-doubt, pride, and old ways of thinking about being strong.

That is what it means to be strong. That should be your source of pride and concept of strength.

Act on removing negative pride and strength so life becomes more manageable. It is significant to note that this advice is not for others, but for your own sake. Lastly, we must be okay with taking "no" for an answer. People are entitled to what they choose to do. We have free will. A lot of people told me "no" when I expected a yes. We have to have reasonable expectations, but not to the point that we become gloomy inside. Do not let rejection be the saw that breaks the chain of connection. Aspire for certainty, yet be content with rejection. I want to add that a "no' is not the final answer. When you finally receive a yes, meet expectations.

Who can do it alone?

Interconnectedness and Relatability

When it comes to our relationships intimately or communally, it is relevant that we hold the eyes of connection. A lot of the issues in nature are due to human self-interest. Self-interest leads to environmental conflict due to the concept of separation it creates. As humans, we separate nature from us. In some ways, we separate emotionally, spiritually, physically, and intellectually from nature. We put nature in turmoil because we see little connection to it. Our eyes can be ego-driven at the sight of differences. We harp on what differences make us better than other species. It builds a sense of superiority and a hierarchical complex. Through this lens of distinction, we come to see maltreatment of the world we should cherish.

Many human and nature conflict issues include pollution, unethical farming, inappropriate hunting practices, physical/psychological harm, etc. Part of combating these troubles is viewing nature as interconnected and related to us. Nature provides the very spaces we occupy. Nature offers the air we breathe and the food we consume. Nature allows the possibilities for us to thrive. We lose sight of such truths when we hold ourselves higher than nature and at the center of our manufactured importance. We are reminded of how valuable our connection is when natural disasters happen. When air/water quality is detrimental to inhalation, food resources are lacking and eliminated, or fields are too scarce for appropriate farming, we can only remember its usefulness.

When we place the importance of reliance on each other (nature and humans), the value of nature becomes greater. I discuss nature and humans not as a way to distinguish, but to increase understanding of interconnectedness. I want us to get to the point that we no longer distinguish humans from nature. Furthermore, we can apply interconnectedness to our human relationships. We all observe the emphasis on differences causing our issues. Whether it be skin, hair, location, personality, language, religion, philosophy, or more, we can become arrogant about our differences. We focus on what makes us unique and place it on a pedestal. Historically, even today, on a mass or individual basis, we observe that other things different from ourselves are inferior or less than us. We must be conscious of ourselves to acknowledge differences not as a competitive advantage, but as something to admire. When it comes to building bonds and maintaining relationships, similarities will go a long way. When we find things that are alike, we are more likely to treat each other better. The similarity is why we may value our friends and family. If we are good people, we will do them no intentional harm, and when we learn about the damage we cause unconsciously, we will seek to stop pushing it. We do this with friends and family because they can be emotionally, spiritually, physically, and intellectually close to us. We focus on what we share. We may depend upon each other for support in a variety of ways. We rely on one another for emotional support, bond, finance, guidance, etc. An exercise we can all practice to bring ourselves closer to one another is making a

list of commonalities we share as people in nature.
Think of all the strangers you have run into. Make a
like of commonalities between yourself and
strangers. Not only will you become amazed at
what makes us similar, but hopefully, we live by
what amazes us. We can also list what makes you
unique and how your uniqueness can improve
someone else's life. We can begin to see each other
differently and more positively. Appreciate
differences and embrace similarities.

How else are we all connected?

About The Author

Dorian Scott Withrow Jr. was born on April 13th, 2000, in Buffalo, New York. His education was primarily through the Amherst Central School District. Dorian began his blossoming in high school by facing and conquering many challenges. His achievements were within many programs he was involved in; programs such as Youth of the Year, Jack and Jill of America, Leadership Buffalo, and Breaking Barriers. He was accepted into Canisius University in 2018 and majored in Animal Behavior Ecology and Conservation (ABEC), with a minor in Philosophy. Throughout university, Dorian was still involved in Breaking Barriers attending meetings, participating in activism, and doing podcasts. He was also involved in his newly found passion, ITF Taekwondo. Dorian graduated from Canisius University in May 2022.

Youth of the Year (Boys and Girls Club)

Youth of the Year is an achievement that youth in Boys and Girls Clubs accomplish for community involvement, leadership, character, and even mentorship for younger people. People who receive this honor not only receive recognition, but have the opportunity to move on to greater milestones. Youth members selected from different Boys and Girls Clubs around the city are offered to take part in different workshops to meet the next stage. These workshops include public speaking, writing, teaching, etc. He did not meet the next stage, but out of six competitors, he came in second.

Jack & Jill Of America

Dorian was also involved in Jack & Jill of America, a program for young black males. The program held many workshops such as leadership, fitness, dress to impress, public speaking, and dance (West African and Urban Ballroom). This program allowed for the creation of a network among its members. Community service was another element of the program to instill the importance of serving exposure to many unique people and aided Dorian in character development. At the end of the program, boys become men through African rights of passage. The final ceremony involved our speeches, dance, and rights of passage. The boys got to give themselves a name when they became men. Dorian became Adwin (thinker and artist).

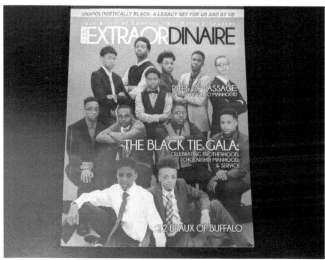

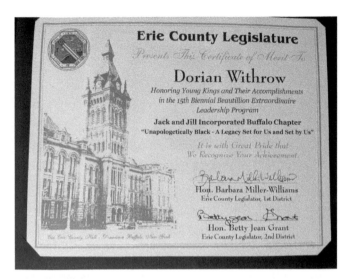

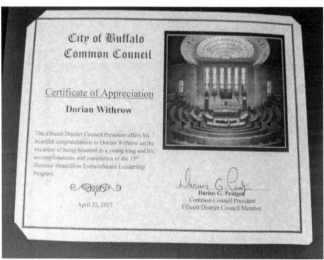

Leadership Buffalo

Leadership Buffalo was a program Dorian experienced during his first retreat. He met a lot of interesting people from special backgrounds. Leadership Buffalo also held a lot of workshops regarding leadership, cooking, dining etiquette (lesson from a former butler of the queen of England), diversity, inclusion, and more. There was an amazing opportunity for teamwork and building more connections.

Honors and Rewards

Dorian received many honors and rewards in high school. Dorian obtained the national honors society for maintaining merit roll in high school. He also attended Harkness Erie One Boces for Animal Science and earned the national technical honor society. Dorian gained scholarships from Buffalo Urban League and Delta Sigma Theta Sorority. Finally, he graduated from high school in 2018 and pursued a bachelor's at Canisius University. Currently, he is a Canisius alumnus with a Bachelor of Science. Dorian had a strong liking for philosophy. His love for philosophy has led him to earn a place in Phi Sigma Tau, a philosophical honor society, and be rewarded with the St. Thomas Aquinas Award in Philosophy for having demonstrated exceptional achievement in philosophy. Lastly, he was granted the Martin Luther King Award for promoting social justice, social harmony, civil rights, human rights, advocacy of the poor, and non-violence.

Dorian is a graduate and still a youth council member of Breaking Barriers, a program in which males of color ages twelve to twenty-four, act on policy, mentoring, leadership, and improving work opportunities and conditions of other young people in education (just to name a few). Dorian gained very valuable knowledge and developed many meaningful connections. Dorian has had the opportunity to become a social justice trainer and continues to engage in the Breaking Barriers podcasts.

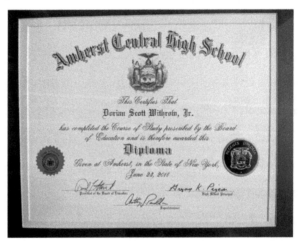

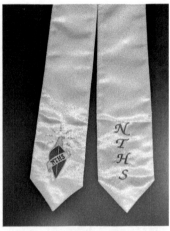

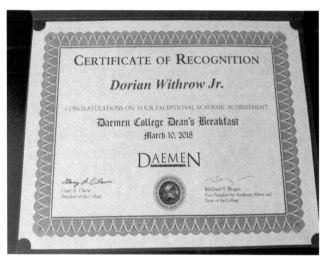

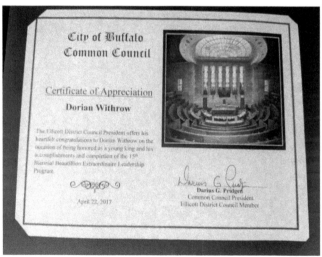

ITF Taekwondo

Dorian is also a martial artist and ITF Taekwondo practitioner. He has some knowledge of Isshin Ryu karate from his grandfather. Dorian started ITF Taekwondo in May 2019. Through diligent and persistent work, he achieved a master's club affiliation. He also takes part in D.E.L.T.A. (Dedicated, Enthusiastic, Loyal, Teaching, Assistant) Team where he can assist in teaching and uplifting others' lives. Dorian is officially an Il-Dan and passionate about further training.

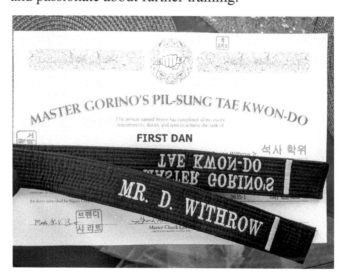

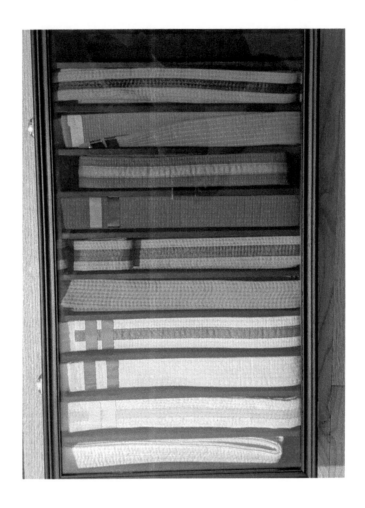

Books Authored By Dorian S.Withrow Jr.

Book Alphabetical

Speak! Young Brown People, Speak. We are listening!
A.L. Savvy Publications 2014, 2022

Thoughts Of Creativity King 114 Realities. Dorian
Withrow Jr., Withrow LLC, Buffalo NY, 2022

Wisdom 45 Advice. Dorian S. Withrow Jr., Withrow
LLC, Buffalo NY, 2022

Conversations You Need. Dorian Withrow Jr., Withrow
LLC, Buffalo NY, 2023